With love and admiration, this book is my tribute to our superman.

Table of Contents

Introduction

Welcome to Dad's Popular Filipino Dishes Cookbook! My name is Donna Mae Mascarinas and I am ecstatic to share this book with you. When my dad unexpectedly passed away on a dreadfully cold and snowy night in 2020, my life, and my family's lives, changed forever. Even now, my memories are life before December 2020 and life after December 2020. Like many Filipino families, mine is tight knit with dad as the vital organ. Without him, we are all a bit lost and taken aback.

I was in so much pain that I welcomed grief and the darkness it brought me. It dictated what I did or didn't do on a daily basis. It dictated what decisions I did or didn't make. My two young children felt the loss of the mother they knew before that cold and tragic night. I isolated myself from my friends. My career suffered. It took all the energy that I had just to get out of bed.

Somehow, I got back on my feet. Time only has one direction, forward. Eventually, the season of my life changed. I began feeling lucid again and became more present for the daily necessities. Then one day, I found peace doing chores that I used to think were boring and mundane in my life pre-December 2020. I found peace in doing our laundry. I found joy in grocery shopping.

I found excitement in cooking again. Grief had broken up with me, but I still had that pit in my stomach that missed my dad so very much.

I found myself naturally gravitating towards cooking dad's home-made dishes. It brought me back to times that I spent feasting on his cuisine and how nurturing it felt. I missed that and wanted it again. That was the hardest reality that I had to accept. The finality of him being gone. I had to learn how to live without our weekly lunches, our long conversations, and hearing him belting to the angels like he was Josh Groban himself.

One day, I brought home freshly baked Pandesal from our local Asian market. It smelled of Christmas morning, our family tradition. My children came home from school and when they smelled the bread, they both made that nasal sound that we all make when we are transcended into a memory of a warm and loving home. My son said, "this smells like papa." My daughter replied, "because this is papa's bread." And that's when I knew. Food was such an integral part of my dad's love language, of course this was the way to reconnect with him. You know that moment when you have an epiphany that is so simple and right in front of you all along? Thus began my culinary exploration into my dad's Filipino recipes.

My dad didn't have a rolodex of recipes, he did not even own a measuring cup or measuring spoons. He cooked with heart and simply smelled and tasted everything. He was a talented chef but recorded nothing. I had to recreate his dishes based on the countless years of sitting at his kitchen counter watching him whistling his favorite tunes while he cooked these amazing dishes. My fondest memory would be coming home to the delicious smells from the kitchen and hearing him whistling tunes of Matt Monro. At potluck parties, I watched people ooh and ahh while clapping their hands when dad would unveil his dishes. He brought so much joy into people's lives this way. I wish to deliver the same happiness to my own family and friends. It is why I am eager to share these same beloved recipes with you. May your Filipino dishes launch a lifetime of loving memories at your kitchen counter.

Author's Notes

While I find Filipino cuisine to be original in its uniquely bold flavors, I celebrate the influences of Spanish and Chinese cuisine. There is a history behind these influences, but I'll leave that story to be told by the history lovers out there.

Savory Filipino foods strive to have a balanced trifecta: sour, sweet, and salty. There are certain ingredients that are available in the Philippines but not easily available here in the United States (unless you shop through Amazon where everything is easily accessible). I have made substitutions for such ingredients that are not in our local grocery stores.

Filipino dishes are usually rustic and served family style.

Tagalog is the language I grew up speaking. It is also the standardized national language in the Philippines. The name of the recipes in this book will be in Tagalog but I will add a loose English translation to describe the dish. I will also share my personal experiences with you about the dishes in hopes of making them more relatable if you are not familiar with them.

I have done my best providing serving size, prepping time, and cooking time for these recipes. Please be forgiving and keep in mind that these are suggestions. Serving sizes for the lumpia, for instance, will vary depending on how much filling you use to make thin or thick eggrolls. Prepping time also will depend on your culinary skill level. I am slow and overly cautious with my knife skills so these times might be longer prep times compared to your Samurai skills. Generally, (from someone who tends to burn things), developing rich flavors in these dishes cannot and should not be rushed. Use your judgement and pay attention to your heat level.

Curiosity and patience are essential traits with learning anything for the first time. Be easy on yourself and enjoy the process. Try not to rush through the experience. Smell everything. Taste everything. It was in the cooking, not the eating, when I experienced the true essence of Filipino cuisine.

Let's get cooking...

Chapter 1

CROWD PLEASING APPETIZERS

In Filipino cuisine, the appetizer dishes for many people will seem like an entree in itself. Typically, appetizers are pre-meal courses to stimulate one's appetite. In the Philippine culture, our appetites need no stimulation. Our palates are never dormant. And our eating habits do not conform to the three-square meal rule. In the Philippine culture, we have what's called "merienda" or snacks, and plenty of it, in between meals. It is not uncommon in my family to discuss the next meal while we are still eating the meal served in front of us on the table!

Sometimes Filipino appetizers are mistaken as side dishes. However, in this book, I honor them as appetizers because they can stand alone with or without the main course. Whatever their category, these dishes are delicious and know how to please a crowd.

Chapter 1

CROWD PLEASING APPETIZERS

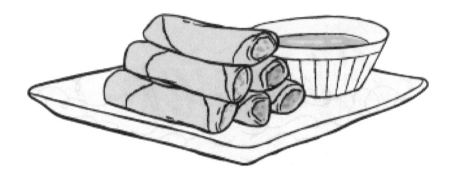

Lumpiang Shanghai (Fried Filipino Eggrolls)

Serves: 50	Prep time for filling: 15 mins	Cook time: 3-5 mins per batch (Size of batch depends on size of fryer.

Lumpia Shanghai (Loom-pee-yah Sh-ang-high), or fried eggroll, is probably the most recognized Filipino dish in America. It is commonly known as Lumpia. If I were to pick three of the most generally recognized Filipino dishes in America, it would be lumpia (eggrolls), pancit (noodles), and chicken adobo. While most Americans generalize lumpia as fried egg rolls or fried spring rolls with a filling of ground pork, beef, chicken, or turkey, or a combination of all these, there are multiple versions of lumpia. There are fried versions with vegetables only or vegetables with shrimp. There are also lumpia that are fresh and not fried.

This is the fried lumpia recipe that I grew up eating, my dad's version of lumpia shanghai.

Don't forget to make the Sweet and Sour dipping sauce! This sauce is essential to balancing out the dry, salty, and savory tones of this dish.

INGREDIENTS

2 ½ pounds ground pork

2 cups yellow onions
(minced)

¼ cup carrots(minced)

¼ cup parsley (minced)

2 eggs

1 teaspoon salt

1 teaspoon garlic powder

½ teaspoon black pepper

1 teaspoon sesame oil

2 cups neutral oil (canola or
vegetable)

50 separated store-bought
lumpia wrapper

DIRECTIONS

1. Add ground pork, onion, carrots, and parsley in a large bowl. Mix until well incorporate.

2. Add eggs, salt, garlic powder, black pepper, and sesame oil. Mix until the ingredients are blended.

3. Take the store-bought lumpia wrappers that may be stuck together and separate them individually. Set aside.

4. See instructions on the next page (page 9) on "How to Roll A Lumpia." Repeat these steps until the filling mixture is completely consumed.

5. Heat oil to 350-375 °F and deep fry until the filling is thoroughly cooked and the exterior turns golden brown. Remove from oil and place vertically in a bowl lined with a paper towel. Be careful not to over crowd fryer. To cook eggrolls evenly, fry them in batches.

6. Plate whole eggrolls, or cut them into two halves, or into your desired size.

7. Serve with homemade sweet and sour (recipe on page 11) and enjoy!

How To Roll A Lumpia

Wrapping lumpia is a technique that takes practice. Before you know it, you will be an eggroll wrapping machine. When you enter a Filipino home, you can always tell when lumpia is on the menu for an upcoming party. The first thing you will hear is the joyful, yet unbashful, light chismis (gossip) from a group of close-knit people who are sitting around the kitchen table. Then, you will see a table filled with plates of separated store-bought eggroll wrappers next to an oversized bowl. From this bowl you will experience the divine scent of deliciously prepared lumpia filling. The tradition of bonding over rolling lumpia is a labor of connection and love. It is the secret ingredient that you can taste with every bite.

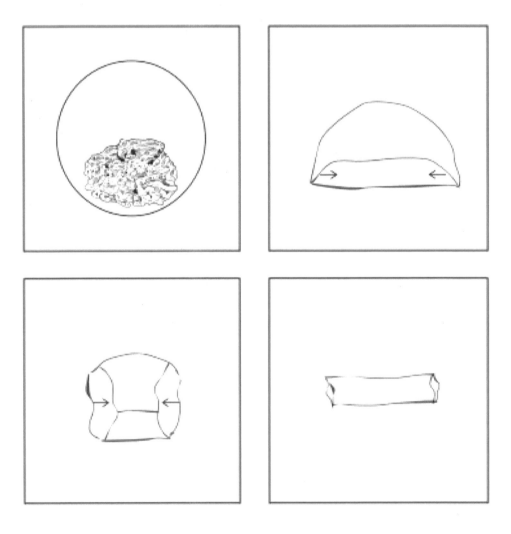

1. Take a heaping tablespoonful of the filling. You will need to rely on your judgment and trial and error with this step because there is not a real measurement here. Also, store-bought eggroll wrappers come in different sizes, so the filling measurement relies on the size that you purchased. If you wish, roll a sample eggroll and deep fry to golden brown. Cut it in half to ensure the filling is thoroughly cooked. If it is, you found the perfect measurement! If raw, consider using less filling. If overcooked or burnt, consider using more filling.

2. Aim to make a nice, elongated line of filling that extends from one edge to the other edge of the wrapper.

3. Roll the wrapper one time towards the middle lightly tucking the edge of the wrapper under the filling.

4. Take each side of the wrapper (where the filling is exposed) and flip each side inward towards the center roll. The filling is completely wrapped with this step.

5. Continue to roll the lumpia until all the wrapper is tightly rolled around the filling.

6. Secure the edge by gluing the edges. Using a brush or the tip of your finger, take a small amount of water or egg wash. I prefer to use water for easier clean up.

Homemade Sweet & Sour Dipping Sauce

Serves: 1   Prep time: 5 mins   Cook time: 15 mins

When eaten by the dozens, Lumpiang Shanghai in time can feel dry and salty. Add balance by using a homemade sweet and sour dipping sauce. There is no shame in using your favorite store-bought dipping sauce either! If you enjoy added heat, spice up this recipe with dashes of your favorite hot sauce or pinches of red pepper flakes.

INGREDIENTS

1 cup canned pineapple juice

1/3 cup rice vinegar

2 tablespoons ketchup

¾ cup brown sugar

2 tablespoons cornstarch

¼ red pepper flakes
(optional for spicy lovers)

DIRECTIONS

1. Use a whisk to mix pineapple juice, rice vinegar, ketchup, brown sugar, and cornstarch in a medium saucepan in low heat. Wait to boil and stir continuously until mixture has loosely thickened or to your desired consistency.

2. Remove from the heat and add dashes of hot sauce or red pepper flakes if you prefer it to be spicy.

3. Serve and enjoy!

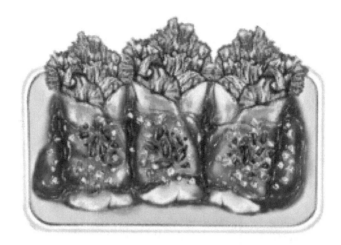

Lumpiang Sariwa (Fresh Filipino Eggrolls)

Serves: 5   Prep time for   Cook time: 30 mins
                 filling: 10 mins

Behind every strong Lumpiang Shanghai is an even stronger Lumpiang Sariwa (Loom-pee-yah Sa-ree-wah). Weighing in a healthier alternative to the deep fried lumpia, Lumpiang Sariwa is a noteworthy competitor. From its soft fresh crepe wrap to the intense garlic sauce that smothers over its entirety, this appetizer is sure to keep the vampires away. The recipe calls for peanut butter spread inside this perfectly invented eggroll. Sounds strange at first but trust me, it is no Sariwa without it. If you are like both my children and are allergic to peanuts, try almond butter as a substitute.

INGREDIENTS

2 tablespoons neutral oil
(canola or vegetable)

1 medium yellow onion
(chopped)

2 cloves garlic (minced)

½ pound ground pork

1 medium potato (small cubes)

1 medium carrot (julienned)

½ cup water

3 ½ ounces firm tofu (small
cubes)

10 prawns (sliced in half)

2 cups cabbage (shredded)

2 tablespoons fish sauce

¼ teaspoon ground black
pepper

5 lumpia wrapper

5 separated green lettuce leaves

1 cup peanut butter or almond
butter

½ cup chopped peanuts (or
almonds if allergic)

DIRECTIONS

1. Heat oil in a medium size pan.
2. Sauté onions until tender and translucent then add garlic.
3. Add ground pork, cook for 3 minutes until lightly browned while breaking it up into small lumps.
4. Add potato, carrots, and water. Let it cook for another 3 minutes or until potatoes are tender.
5. Add tofu, cook for 3 minutes or until the edges of the tofu are lightly golden.
6. Add prawns and cook for 3 minutes until it is pink and opaque.
7. Add cabbage, fish sauce, and pepper. Cook for a few minutes more just until the cabbage is tender. To remove any extra fluid, place the cooked filling in a colander. Set aside and let it cool.
8. Place the lumpia wrapper on a plate and place a lettuce leaf on top with the curly part of the leaf lightly exposed on one side of the wrapper. Spread a thin layer of peanut butter or almond butter over the leaf and on the eggroll if the leaf doesn't cover it entirely.
9. See page 9 on "How To Roll A Lumpia." Follow these instructions but leave the side with exposed lettuce open and unwrapped.
10. Ladle the homemade garlic sauce on top of the lumpia and garnish with a sprinkle of chopped peanuts or almonds.
11. Serve and enjoy!

Homemade Wrapper for Lumpiang Sariwa

Serves: 5   Prep time: 2 mins   Cook time: 5 mins

Try making homemade wrapper. Accept this challenge for bragging rights!

INGREDIENTS

¼ cup all-purpose flour

½ cup cornstarch

1 teaspoon white sugar

¼ teaspoon salt

2 eggs

½ tablespoon neutral oil
(canola or vegetable)

1 cup milk

DIRECTIONS

1. Mix flour, cornstarch, sugar, salt, (all the dry ingredients), in a bowl.

2. Mix eggs, oil, milk, (all the wet) ingredients, in separate bowl.

3. Make a well in the dry ingredients then add the half wet ingredients into the dry ingredients. Whisk to combine. Then add the remaining half of the wet ingredients while whisking continuously. I find this technique helpful in preventing lumps.

4. Heat a 9" non-stick pan over low heat. Spray or brush the pan with a little amount of oil.

5. Pour ½ cup of the mixture into the pan and swirl to spread the mixture thin and evenly. Cook for 1 minute or until the wrapper is no longer liquid and no longer sticks to the pan. Flip and cook the other side for 10 seconds. The wrapper should be thin, moist, and foldable. It is overcooked if it is dry, crispy, and cracks when you fold it.

6. It' is ready for use. Happy assembling!

Homemade Garlic Sauce for Lumpiang Sariwa

Serves: 1   Prep time: 3 mins   Cook time: 5 mins

INGREDIENTS

2 cups water

4 big cloves garlic
(minced)

½ teaspoon salt

1/3 cup brown sugar

1 tablespoon soy sauce

2 tablespoons cornstarch
(dissolved in ¼ cup
water)

DIRECTIONS

1. Mix water, garlic, salt, sugar, and soy sauce in a saucepan and bring it to a soft boil over medium to low heat, then let it cook for 3 minutes.

2. In a cup, dissolve cornstarch into water.

3. Add liquid cornstarch into simmering sauce while whisking until the sauce becomes loosely thick or your desired consistency.

4. Ladle over the Lumpiang Sariwa and enjoy!

Crab & Corn Egg Drop Soup

Serves: 8   Prep time: 5 mins   Cook time: 25 mins

The state of Louisiana has their traditional crab and corn bisque, New England has their crab and corn chowder, Filipino's have crab and corn egg drop soup. Crab and corn are as classically paired as garlic and rice. This recipe is our version of the Chinese egg drop soup. I have made this soup with more flare by garnishing it with crispy bacon or even adding potatoes as an ingredient. However, I find that my attempts to enhance this dish takes away from its already perfect character.

INGREDIENTS

¼ cup butter

¼ cup all-purpose flour

2 cups whole milk

2 cups half-and-half

1 ¾ cups whole kernel corn
(frozen or canned)

1 cup green onions (chopped)

1 pounds fresh crab meat

½ teaspoon salt

½ teaspoon ground white
pepper

1 tablespoon soy sauce

2 eggs

¼ cup flatleaf parsley
(chopped)

1/2 teaspoon ground black
pepper

DIRECTIONS

1. Melt butter in a deep pot, add flour, and mix until incorporated. This should take less than one minute, do not burn the flour.

2. Add milk gradually while continuing to stir using a whisk to prevent lumps. Then, add half and half and switch to a ladle or wooden spoon to gently stir.

3. Add corn, green onions, and cook for a few minutes until warmed through.

4. Add crabmeat, salt, pepper, soy sauce, and simmer until small bubbles form around the edge, do not let it boil.

5. Crack eggs into a bowl and scramble. Swirl the soup around the pot to create flow while gently pouring the egg a little at a time. Watch the egg cook as thin elongated shapes. Continue to stir for at least one minute for the egg drops to cook.

6. Serve piping hot in a bowl.

7. Garnish with chopped fresh parsley then ground black pepper and enjoy!

Chicken Empanada

Serves: 8   Prep time for   Cook time: 25 mins
                filling: 5 mins

Empanada (Em-pah-nah-dah) is a half-circle shaped pastry pocket with a filling. In this recipe, we are making a savory empanada that is essentially a petite meat pie. Empanadas are crispy and flaky, portable and convenient like a sandwich, and is a flavorful comfort food. Fill it with ground beef, only vegetables, mixed seafood, or even cheese.

Although it requires a little more effort in the kitchen, I love how empanadas can transform your leftovers into an entirely new dish. Take leftover chicken and shred it for your empanada filling, for example. As with rolling lumpia, this dish also requires a labor of love. Similarly, it is well worth the sweat equity. Have fun with the construction of your empanadas. How you decide to seal your edges will become your signature stamp to this dish!

Do not be afraid to take a short cut by using store-bought pastry dough. If you are ever up for the challenge, make your own pastry dough someday. But, no pressure!

INGREDIENTS

2 tablespoons neutral oil
(canola or vegetable)

1 cup yellow onion (chopped)

1 cup potato (small cubes)

½ pound chicken breast fillet
(boiled or roasted then
shredded)

1 cup red bell pepper (small
cubes)

1 cup carrots (small cubes)

½ cup water

½ teaspoon salt

¼ teaspoon ground pepper

1 cup green peas

½ cup raisins

DIRECTIONS

1. Heat oil in a pan over medium heat.
2. Sauté onions until soft and translucent.
3. Add potatoes then cover until potatoes are half cooked.
4. Add the shredded chicken, red bell pepper, carrots mix until blended.
5. Add the water then salt and pepper. Stir until liquid is almost evaporated.
6. Add green peas and raisins and cook for 2-3 or minutes until liquid is fully evaporated and mixture is dry.
7. To remove any extra fluid, place the cooked filling in a colander. Set aside and let it cool.
8. Use a large round cookie cutter or knife to cut empanada dough into 16 round pieces.
9. Spoon enough empanada fillings in the center of the dough disk. Fold half towards the edges and pinch the sides to secure. Use a fork to press and seal the sides of the dough. See also "How To Fold An Empanada" on page 22.
10. Put the empanadas on a baking sheet lined with parchment paper in a single layer.
11. Preheat oven for 350 °F.
12. Using the egg wash, brush each empanada to make them shiny and brown after baking.
13. Using toothpick or fork, prick 3-5 small holes on each empanadas to let the steam out and prevent them from bursting open while baking.
14. Bake for 20 minutes at 350°F or until the dough is cooked through and is light brown and shiny.

Homemade Dough for Empanada

INGREDIENTS

3 cups flour

½ teaspoon baking powder

4 tablespoons sugar

½ tablespoon salt

1 cup cold unsalted butter
(small cubes)

6-10 tablespoons cold water

DIRECTIONS

1. Combine the flour, baking powder, sugar, and salt in the bowl of a food processor and pulse for one minute or until blended.

2. Add butter and lightly pulse until it resembles coarse meal with a few pea-size pieces of butter remaining.

3. Pulse while adding one tablespoon of water at a time until dough can hold together and is no longer in crumbles.

4. Remove the dough and form into a ball. Cut the ball into 4 equal parts.

5. Roll each cut dough then use a floured roller to flatten dough into 1/2" thickness.

6. Use a large round cookie cutter or knife to cut 2 round pieces from each flattened portion. Each 1/4 of the ball yields 2 empanada wrappers.

7. You will have 8 wrappers to make 8 empanadas. Enjoy!

How To Fold An Empanada

1. In a bowl, separate egg whites and whisk.

2. Take 3 tablespoons of empanada filling and fill to the edge of the wrapper.

3. Brush the filling side edges with egg whites.

4. Fold over to enclose filling and press to seal.

5. Crimp with a fork or hand pleat like you would the edge of a pie crust to seal the empanada and decorate the edge.

LONG LIFE NOODLES DISHES

Another well-known savory dish in Filipino cuisine is "pancit" or noodles.

I remember dad always making the longest of noodle dishes whenever it was someone's birthday. If the noodle was a short noodle, the dish did not make the cut. Noodles represented life. Long noodles meant long life. If only the wives of Henry the 8th knew of this life hack? (Sorry, bad joke. I couldn't resist).

Chapter 2

LONG LIFE NOODLES DISHES

Pancit Bihon (Stir Fry Thin Rice Noodles)

Serves: 6 Prep time: 15 mins Cook time: 20 mins

Bihon (Bee-hawn) is a thin rice noodle. The beauty about this noodle is that it has a fast-cooking time. Using one pan or wok, stir fry ingredients then add this noodle for a quick and easy scrumptious meal. Garnish this with wedges of lemon to brighten the simple flavors. Keep this dish in your back pocket for when you are in a pinch for time.

Do not let the long ingredients list fool you. After making this dish for the first time, make it again, but with your edits. Make this dish again and again while adjusting the recipe each time to fit your mood, preferences, and how quickly you want to feast.

INGREDIENTS

3 tablespoons neutral oil
(canola or vegetable)

1 medium yellow onion
(chopped)

2 cloves garlic (minced)

½ pound pork belly (small,
thin slices)

½ pound shrimp (deveined)

2 medium carrots (small
strips)

6 green beans (diagonal
strips)

1 medium red bell pepper
(strips)

½ cup celery stalk (chopped)

1 small cabbage
(shredded)

4 tablespoons soy sauce

½ teaspoon ground pepper

3-4 cups water

1 chicken or shrimp bouillon
or 1 tablespoon vegetable or
chicken seasoning

8 ounces rice noodles

1 lemon (wedges)

DIRECTIONS

1. Heat oil in a pan.

2. Sauté onion and garlic in neutral oil over medium to high heat until onion is soft and translucent.

3. Add the pork until cooked and tender then add the shrimp until it is pink and opaque. Remove the shrimp and set aside to not overcook them.

4. Add carrots and green beans, cook for 2 minutes. Stir until almost tender.

5. Add the red bell pepper, celery, and cabbage cook for another 2 minutes. Stir until blended.

6. Add soy sauce, ground pepper, and water. Continue stirring. Let simmer until vegetables are tender but still crisp.

7. Remove the mixed ingredients from the pan but leave the liquid juices. Add shrimp or chicken bouillon or seasoning to the liquids and stir until dissolved.

8. Add the noodles to the liquid. Stir and simmer until noodles absorb the liquid and become soft. You may add more water if noodles are still hard when liquids are fully evaporated.

9. Return the shrimp and cooled mixture you set and incorporate with noodles.

10. Transfer to a serving plate and garnish with wedges of lemon. Enjoy!

Pancit Canton (Filipino Chow Mein)

Serves: 4   Prep time: 10 mins Cook time: 20 mins

Canton (Cun-ton) noodles are versatile egg noodles that have a springy texture. Pancit Canton is the Filipino version of Chow Mein.

INGREDIENTS

2 tablespoons neutral oil (canola or vegetable)

2 cloves garlic (minced)

1 medium yellow onion (chopped)

½ pound chicken breast fillet (cubed)

10 prawns (deveined)

3 tablespoons soy sauce

2 tablespoons oyster sauce

1 big carrot (julienned)

1 big bell pepper (julienned)

1 cup snow peas (ends trimmed)

1 stalk celery (chopped)

1- 1 ½ cup water

1 cube chicken bouillon or 1 tablespoon chicken seasoning

½ small cabbage (shredded)

1 tablespoon cornstarch

½ - 1 teaspoon ground pepper

1 packet of canton noodles or 250 grams

DIRECTIONS

1. Heat oil in a pan.
2. Sauté garlic and onion until the onion is tender and translucent.
3. Add chicken, cook for 3-5 minutes or when chicken is warmed through, if it's left over chicken. Or 3-5 minutes or when the chicken is cooked through, if chicken is raw.
4. Add shrimp and cook until pink and opaque.
5. Adjust the heat to low and pour in soy sauce and oyster sauce and stir until well blended.
6. Add the carrots, bell pepper, snow peas, celery and mix. Cook for about 1 minute, careful not to overcook the vegetables.
7. Adjust the heat to high and pour in one cup of water, chicken bouillon or other preferred seasoning. Once it simmers, stir in cabbage and cook for a few seconds.
8. Transfer all the mixed ingredients in a bowl leaving only the liquids in the pan.
9. In a separate cup, dissolve the starch in the remaining ½ cup of water.
10. Into the hot pan, add ground pepper and corn starch liquid. Stir until liquid is thick with the consistency of a loose sauce.
11. Add noodles to the liquid and loosen them so every surface touches the sauce and has a chance to cook. Add water as needed if sauce dries.
12. Add back the meat and vegetables, stir to combine and then turn off the heat.
13. Garnish with lemon wedges and enjoy!

Pancit Sotanghon Soup (Mung Bean Noodle Soup)

Serves: 4   Prep time: 20 mins Cook time: 22 mins

Sotanghon (So-tang-hung) noodles are transparent noodles made of mung beans. These noodles are also known as vermicelli, crystal, or glass noodles.

This is my daughter's favorite noodle dish because of its smooth and slippery texture. I take it as a positive sign of approval when I see her wiping her messy cheeks from slurping these noodles. Every time she sees a pancit dish, she will ask if it is the slippery kind? Her disappointment is palpable when the dish is not Sotanghon noodles.

If you are up for an adventurous noodle dish, this is a must try. I have seen this version made with canned sardines. For my children's picky palates however, I make it with chicken.

INGREDIENTS

7 cups water

1 ½ pound chicken breast

1 dry bay leaves

3 tablespoons neutral oil
(canola or vegetable)

1 medium yellow onion
(chopped)

5 cloves garlic (minced)

2 stalks celery (chopped)

1 chicken bouillon or chicken

1 tablespoon chicken seasoning

1 teaspoon fish sauce or to taste

2 tablespoons annatto powder
(grounded spice to give a
natural red food coloring)

2 ½ ounces sotanghon noodles

1 medium carrot (julienne)

½ small cabbage shredded

1 teaspoon ground black
pepper

2 scallions (chopped)

DIRECTIONS

1. Boil water in a big pot.

2. Add chicken and bay leaf. Cover and boil in medium heat for 20 minutes.

3. Remove chicken from the pot and set aside to cool down. Save the chicken stock.

4. Once the chicken has cooled down, shred the chicken and set aside.

5. In a separate large pot, heat oil.

6. Sauté onions until soft and translucent.

7. Add garlic, celery, and shredded chicken then sauté for 2 minutes to soften vegetables.

8. Into this large pot, pour chicken stock from the chicken breast and bay leaf. Let it boil.

9. Add chicken bouillon or seasoning, fish sauce, and annatto powder and stir.

10. Add sotanghon noodles, then cover the pot. Cook for 10 minutes until noodles are soft and tender.

11. Add carrots and cabbage and cook for 5 minutes until carrots are just tender.

12. Add fish sauce.

13. Garnish with chopped scallions and ground pepper.

14. Serve steaming hot and enjoy!

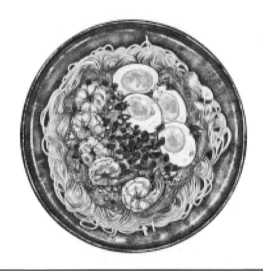

Pancit Palabok
(Thick Rice Noodles in Shrimp Sauce)

Serves: 6   Prep time: 10 mins Cook time: 30 mins

Like Bihon, Palabok (Pala-book) is a type of rice noodle. A thicker version of Bihon, these noodles are delicate and absorb sauces very well. This is a very technical dish compared to the other pancit recipes. Thus, I usually only see this dish at celebratory parties. This was the very dish that won the applause from the crowd with ooh's and aah's upon dad's reveal at one of our large family gatherings. Dad would decorate the top of this dish with alternating rows of sliced boiled egg, crushed chicharron (pig skin chips), and prawns. This dish is truly a piece of art and is noteworthy of the front cover of this book. Ooh and aah indeed!

INGREDIENTS

1 pack bihon rice noodles
or 500 grams

2 tablespoons neutral oil
(canola or vegetable)

½ pound ground pork

1 cup shrimp or chicken broth

1 shrimp bouillon or 1
tablespoon shrimp seasoning

6 tablespoons all-purpose flour

1 tablespoon anatto powder (if
available or omit from recipe)

2 tablespoons fish sauce

½ teaspoon ground black
pepper

½ pound cooked prawns
(boiled or steamed)

2 boiled eggs (sliced into thin
pieces)

¼ cup green onion or scallions
(finely chopped)

2 lemons (sliced)

Ingredients for fried garlic
topping:

3 tablespoons neutral oil
(canola or vegetable)

1 whole head of garlic (largely
minced)

DIRECTIONS

1. Submerge and soak the rice noodles in a bowl of room temperature water for about 20 minutes. Remove noodles and set aside saving the water for later use.

2. Make fried garlic topping. Heat oil and garlic in a pan. Cook for 2 minutes or until garlic is lightly browned. Remove from heat and put on a plate lined with paper towel. Careful, nobody wants to eat bitter burnt garlic. Watch cooking time as they burn easily.

3. In the same pan, add ground pork. Cook for 5 to 7 minutes until brown breaking it up into lumps. Set aside on plate lined with paper towel.

4. In a medium saucepan, add shrimp or chicken broth and shrimp bouillon or seasoning. Wisk or stir and dissolve powder in the broth. Simmer for 3 minutes.

5. Ladle out a cup of this simmering liquid in a separate cup or bowl. Dissolve the flour and Annatto powder in it.

6. In the simmering saucepan, add the fish sauce, ground black pepper, and liquid with flour and Annatto powder. Lightly boil until the sauce becomes thick. Stir frequently to not burn the bottom of the pan. Turn off the heat.

7. Add cooked ground pork into the sauce and mix. Set aside.

8. Take the pot with noodle water and heat to a boil.

9. Add noodles and boil for 10-15 minutes until tender.

10. Strain the noodles from the boiling water and discard the liquid.

11. Place the noodles on a serving plate. Assemble this dish.

12. Add the sauce on top of the noodles then arrange the toppings of cooked shrimp, sliced boiled eggs, fried garlic, and green scallions above the sauce.

13. Garnish with lemon wedges and enjoy!

Chapter 3

EAT YOUR VEGETABLES

Filipino cuisine is mostly celebrated for its meat dishes. However, I find our vegetable dishes to be equally intriguing. Our vegetable dishes are so vibrant and satisfying, they can easily take center stage as the main entrée of any meal. I will confess that I am a late bloomer when it comes to enjoying these dishes. I was a meat and rice kind of gal as a child. Now in adulthood, I finally appreciate why my parents told me to "eat your vegetables." These vegetable dishes are truly distinctive dishes!

EAT YOUR VEGETABLES

Ginataang Pinakbet (Coconut Vegetable Stew)

Serves: 4   Prep time: 20 mins   Cook time: 22 mins

Pinakbet (Pin-ak-bet) is a traditional vegetable medley stew seasoned with Bagoong (Bah-go-ong) or shrimp paste. Bagoong has a pungent smell and flavor and is an acquired taste. Unfortunately for my children, they have not learned to love it yet. As an alternative, I make Ginataang Pinakbet. Rather than relying on Bagoong shrimp paste for taste, I use coconut milk or Ginataang (Ghee-nah-ta-an) with fish sauce.

The secret to this recipe is to not overcook the vegetables. Let the green beans keep some crunch for a fresher eating experience. Over cooking the okra will give this dish a slimy finish so carefully cook the whole okra so it remains intact. On the other hand, squash is delicious when melted into simmering coconut milk. Sometimes, I'll even squish a squash cube, or two, to help thicken the sauce and to give it a deeper flavor.

This is a trial-and-error type of dish so have fun with it!

INGREDIENTS

2 tablespoons neutral oil (canola or vegetable)

1 thumb ginger (minced)

1 medium yellow onion (chopped)

4 cloves garlic (crushed)

½ pound medium squid

½ small squash (cubed)

2 cups coconut milk

½ pound fresh okra

6 green beans (cut into 2-inch length)

2 Japanese eggplant (chunks in 4-6 pieces)

1 teaspoon fish sauce or more to taste

¼ teaspoon ground black pepper

DIRECTIONS

1. Heat oil in a medium size pan.

2. Sauté ginger and onion until the onions are soft and translucent. Add garlic.

3. Add the squid and sauté for 2 minutes or until squid is opaque and firm. Remove the squid and set aside after.

4. Add the squash and sauté for 3 minutes.

5. Pour the coconut milk into the pot, let it boil then cover the pot to simmer for 10 minutes.

6. Add okra, green beans, and eggplant. Mix and cook for 8 minutes or until the vegetables are just almost cooked through.

7. Add cooked squid, fish sauce, and ground black pepper, cook for 5 minutes.

8. If the sauce is not thick enough to your preference, squish some of the squash cubes into the sauce to help it thicken. Another way to thicken the liquid is to add more simmering time to evaporate more liquid. Careful not to overcook the vegetables.

9. Serve hot and enjoy!

Ginisang Ampalaya (Sautéed Bitter Melon)

Serves: 4   Prep time: 15 mins   Cook time: 15 mins

Ginisang (Ghee-ni-sah-ang) is to sauté or stir fry. Ampalaya (Am-pah- lah-yeah), or bitter melon, is popular for its distinctive bitter taste and looks like a wrinkled cucumber but has a more vibrant and brighter green color. This dish took me some time to admire. But once you flip over, you will love the distinct bitterness of the melon and will be a fan for life.

Of dad's dishes, my mom craves this dish often. She is always overjoyed when she finds it in the menu in Chinese restaurants. My dad loved to cook for my mom. They were remarkably married for 49 years, together for much longer! Mom's secret to a happy long marriage should be the sequel to this book.

Beware. When cooked improperly, Ampalaya has an overbearing bitter taste. Give it grace. Once you perfect cooking this dish, and I have faith that you will, invite mom over to dinner!

INGREDIENTS

2 pieces ampalaya (thin slices)

1/2 teaspoon salt

2 ½ cups warm water

3 tablespoons neutral oil
(canola or vegetable)

1 tablespoon garlic (minced)

1 medium yellow onion
(sliced)

1 small tomato (sliced)

½ teaspoon ground black
pepper or more to taste

2 eggs

DIRECTIONS

1. Half the ampalaya by slicing it down the middle. Remove the inside core and seeds with a spoon. Put down the now half and emptied ampalaya with cut side down forming a hollow tunnel on your cutting board. Cut into thin pieces that form a "c" shape and place in a large bowl. Add salt and lukewarm water then soak for 10 minutes. Drain and rinse after and set aside.

2. Heat oil in a medium sized pan.

3. Sauté onion until soft and translucent. Add garlic and tomato and sauté until tomato is soft.

4. Add the ampalaya, salt, and pepper.

5. In a separate bowl, beat eggs. Slowly pour into the hot pan while mixing all contents together. If you don't slowly add the eggs while mixing all the ingredients in the pan, this dish will turn into an omelet dish.

6. Serve and enjoy!

Ginisang Munggo Soup
(Mung Bean Noodle Soup)

Serves: 6   Prep time: 10 mins Cook time: 1 hour

Munggo (Mung-go) Soup is a soup made of mung beans, a type of legume. Mung beans are little round hard green beans, smaller than a pea. They are purchased dried but when boiled into a soup, it cracks open and leaves a lentil soup type of consistency. Traditionally, this recipe uses small servings of fried pork belly (Lechon) or small chunks from deep fried pork knuckle (Krispy Pata). I tend to use ground pork for convenience and for a healthier option. Ladle this hot bean soup over a bowl of steaming hot rice and call it a perfect night in!

INGREDIENTS

3 cups water

2 tablespoons neutral oil
(canola or vegetable)

½ pound ground pork

1 ½ cups mung beans

2 garlic cloves

1 medium tomato (chopped)

1 medium yellow onion
(chopped)

2 tablespoons fish sauce

2 cups fresh spinach

1 cup store-bought
chicharron or pork rinds

¼ teaspoon ground black
pepper

DIRECTIONS

1. Boil water in a large pot.

2. Add munggo beans and cook until beans are soft, between 40-45 minutes or as directed on the package instructions.

3. In a separate pan, heat oil and sauté onion until soft and translucent. Add garlic and tomato until tomato is soft.

4. Add ground pork and cook through while breaking apart into small lumps.

5. To the cooked and simmering munggo beans, add the sauteed contents and fish sauce and simmer for 10 minutes.

6. Stir. If needed, add more water as needed until you reach a slightly loose stew consistency.

7. Add fresh spinach and allow 1 minute for it to wilt.

8. Garnish with chicharron and ground pepper.

9. Serve and enjoy!

Tortang Talong (Eggplant Omelette)

Serves: 1   Prep time: 25 mins Cook time: 6 mins

While most of our vegetable dishes can stand alone as a main entrée course, this one may need a lead actor. Our fellow vegetarians may disagree with me because this is an Oscar worthy dish. Tortang (Tort-ang) Talong (Ta-long) is a flattened roasted eggplant that is dipped into scrambled eggs and fried into an eggplant fritter or an eggplant omelet. If I served this alone as a meal to my family, they would look around the table asking: "where's the meat?" However, try this recipe for yourself. Let me know if it is a side dish or an entrée?

INGREDIENTS

1 Japanese eggplant

¼ teaspoon salt

½ teaspoon ground
black pepper

1 egg

¼ cup neutral oil (canola
or vegetable)

DIRECTIONS

1. Cook the eggplant directly on a gas stovetop fire on low or on a grill until the skin of the eggplant turns brown to black. It will look burnt. Make sure to continuously rotate the eggplant until all the skin of the eggplant appear brown and burnt.

2. Set aside and let the eggplant cool down. When it is safe on your fingers, peel the burnt skin layer off from the eggplant keeping its cooked core intact.

3. Place eggplant on a plate. Flatten using a fork. Salt and pepper on both sides.

4. In a separate bowl, beat egg.

5. Dip the eggplant into the egg mixture.

6. Heat oil in a pan.

7. Fry one side of the eggplant until medium brown.

8. Pour the remaining egg mixture on top of the eggplant and cook for an additional 1 minute to let it set.

9. Turn it over and fry the other side until it gets light to medium brown or when eggs are cooked through.

10. Serve on a wide plate. Enjoy!

Chapter 4

SMELLS LIKE HOME CHICKEN DISHES

Nothing screams dads home cooking like chicken does. I can remember enjoying my days of having chicken pox because it meant that I got to stay home from school and feast on dads' chicken arroz caldo. Or coming home from a cold and wet softball practice to melt into his bowl of tinolang manok. I also remember being mesmerized when watching dad butcher a whole chicken. He would start with sharpening his knife (while showing off how he did this) then effortlessly butchering proportionate pieces like a pro. He would explain how much more cost efficient buying a whole chicken was and how half the fun was in butchering it. Today, I use the same knife skills that he taught me many years ago.

Chapter 4

SMELLS LIKE HOME CHICKEN DISHES

Chicken Adobo
(Chicken Stewed in Vinegar & Soy Sauce)

Serves: 4   Prep time: 5 mins   Cook time: 45 mins

Nothing says Filipino food more than our famous chicken adobo. However, there is a hidden treasure that is often overlooked by many people. With chicken adobo comes left over chicken adobo. With left over chicken adobo is chicken adobo fried rice. Like many stews, flavors only get better with time. Chicken adobo is no different. Try it for yourself!

Heat a pan with oil then add white rice. When warmed, add left over chicken with its adobo juices containing garlic and bay leaves. Mix until the juices cook into the rice. Once you have dry rice, which is now brown from all the left-over goodness, serve.

Absolutely. Heavenly.

INGREDIENTS

3 tablespoons neutral oil
(canola or vegetable)

2 pounds chicken (cut into
parts)

8 cloves garlic (crushed)

1 medium yellow onion
(sliced)

5 tablespoons white vinegar

3 tablespoons soy sauce

1 teaspoon whole black
pepper

5 dried bay leaves (whole)

2 cups water

DIRECTIONS

1. Heat oil in a large pot.

2. Add the chicken and cook and rotate for 2 minutes or until it turns light brown in color.

3. Add onion sauté for 1 minute until onion is soft and translucent. Add garlic and let soften.

4. Pour vinegar and bring it to a boil. Then cover and cook on medium heat for 3 minutes.

5. Add soy sauce, whole black pepper, dried bay leaves, and water. Bring it to another boil then cover and simmer for 30 minutes or until the chicken cooked through and is tender.

6. Relish the aroma while this dish comes together. Serve and feast!

Filipino Yellow Chicken Curry

Serves: 4   Prep time: 15 mins Cook time: 45 mins

Growing up, this was the only curry dish that I knew. It wasn't until college that I realized that curries came in all sorts of colors and flavor profiles. The variations of different types of curries intrigues me. From Indian to Thai cuisine, curry dishes fascinate me. However many that I have the opportunity to taste and admire, I find myself going back to dad's yellow chicken curry. There is a familiarity to his dish that always leads me home.

INGREDIENTS

4 tablespoons neutral oil (canola or vegetable)

2 ½ pounds chicken (cut into serving pieces)

2 medium yellow onions (chopped)

1 medium tomato (cubed)

3 cloves garlic (chopped)

1 inch ginger (minced)

32 ounces or 2 pounds of chicken stock

1 ½ teaspoons fish sauce

1 cube chicken bouillon or 1 tablespoon chicken seasoning

1 ½ tablespoons yellow curry powder

4 medium carrots (1 inch)

2 big potatoes (cubed)

2 red bell pepper (sliced into squares)

10 green beans (1 inch)

2 cups coconut milk

¼ teaspoon ground black pepper or more to taste

1 tablespoon red pepper flakes

DIRECTIONS

1. Heat oil in a large pot.
2. Add the chicken and cook and rotate for 2 minutes or until it turns light brown in color.
3. Sauté onion and tomato. Cook until tomato is soft and onion translucent.
4. Add garlic and ginger. Let garlic turn soft or light brown.
5. Pour in chicken stock and bring to a boil.
6. Add fish sauce, chicken bouillon or seasoning, and yellow curry powder stirring until the powder and bullion completely dilute in the stock.
7. Add the cooked chicken into the pot. Cover and cook in medium heat for 30 to 35 minutes until cooked.
8. Add carrots and potato. Cover the pot and continue to cook for 5-8 minutes or until the potatoes are soft and carrots are just tender.
9. Add red bell pepper and green beans and cook for 2 minutes or until green beans are just tender.
10. Add coconut milk and ground black pepper to taste, then mix. Note: In the canned coconut milk, there is a dense part that is white and thick and there is the juice part which is lighter and translucent. If you can separate the two, try only using the dense white part of the coconut milk in this dish and save the juice for another dish.
11. Add red pepper flakes for spicy.
12. Serve and enjoy!

Tinolang Manok (Filipino Chicken Soup)

Serves: 4   Prep time: 15 mins   Cook time: 45 mins

Americans have their coveted chicken soup, I have dads Tinolang (Tin-o-la-ang) Manok (Ma-no-k). The chunks of chayote (chi-yo-te) or green papaya makes this a dish of substance and heft. When chicken and ginger are simmered low and slow, the final soup is what romantic rom coms are made of.

INGREDIENTS

3 tablespoons neutral oil (canola or vegetable)

3 pounds chicken (cut into serving pieces)

5 cloves garlic (chopped)

1 medium yellow onion (chopped)

3 thumbs ginger (julienne)

2 tablespoons fish sauce

32 ounces or 2 pounds of chicken stock

2 green papaya (1 inch wedges)

1 cube chicken bouillon or 1 tablespoon chicken seasoning

¼ teaspoon ground black pepper or more to taste

1 ½ cup malunggay leaves or spinach leaves (fresh or frozen) if not available

DIRECTIONS

1. Heat oil in a large pot.
2. Add the chicken and cook and rotate for 2 minutes or until it turns light brown in color.
3. Add garlic, onion, and ginger until the onion is soft and translucent.
4. Pour the fish sauce and stir.
5. Add chicken stock then bring to a boil. Let boil for 30 minutes when chicken is fully cooked and tender.
6. Meanwhile, prepare the green papaya by peeling its outer skin, then cut in half, then in half again, then into small 1-inch wedges.
7. Add the green papaya wedges into the boiling pot. Bring to a simmer for 15-20 minutes or until papaya is softened.
8. Add chicken bouillon or seasoning and ground black pepper, stir.
9. Turn off the heat and then add the malunggay leaves or spinach leaves into the cooking pot. Cover for 2 minutes. (If you have malunggay leaves available, simply prepare ahead of time by pulling the leaves off the thin branches, rinse, and set aside until it is time to add to this recipe.)
10. Serve and enjoy!

Arroz Caldo (Filipino Rice Porridge)

Serves: 5   Prep time: 5 mins   Cook time: 50 mins

Arroz (ar-roz) Caldo (kal-do) is Spanish for broth rice. In Tagalog, it is known as Lugaw (Loo-gow). This dish is rice soup, or rice porridge, or congee in Chinese cuisine. It is my favorite remedy when I feel under the weather. This dish is light to eat yet satiating to the belly. I love to garnish it with freshly cracked brown pepper, a splash of soy sauce, and a squeeze of lemon. I have seen this dish silence a busy table by replacing loud conversations with hungry slurping sounds.

INGREDIENTS

3 tablespoons neutral oil (canola or vegetable)

2 pounds chicken (cut into serving pieces)

4 cloves garlic (chopped)

1 medium yellow onion (diced)

3 thumbs ginger (minced)

1 cup short grained arborio rice or any glutinous rice

2 pounds of chicken stock

1 cube chicken bouillon or 1 tablespoon chicken seasoning

2-3 tablespoons fish sauce

¼ teaspoon ground black pepper

½ cup scallions (chopped)

4 hard-boiled eggs

Ingredients for fried garlic topping:

3 tablespoons neutral oil (canola or vegetable)

1 whole head of garlic (largely minced)

DIRECTIONS

1. Heat oil in a large pot.

2. Add the chicken and cook and rotate for 2 minutes or until it turns light brown in color.

3. Add garlic, onion, and ginger until the onion is soft and translucent.

4. Add the glutinous rice to the pot and cook for 1 minute. Do not burn the rice. If burnt, do not continue with the recipe and start over.

5. Pour the chicken stock into the pot. Bring to a boil then adjust heat to medium to allow ingredients to cook for 35-40 minutes.

6. Add the chicken bouillon or seasoning, stir, and cover. Continue in medium heat stirring time to time until the rice absorbs the water and the texture becomes porridge-like. Add water if it gets too thick.

7. Add fish sauce, and ground black pepper, then stir and cook for another 3 minutes.

8. Chicken should be cooked through and tender. If not, add more cooking time and water if it gets too thick.

9. Make the fried garlic topping: In a separate small pan, heat oil and add garlic. Cook for 2 minutes or until garlic is lightly browned. Remove from heat and put on a plate lined with paper towel. Careful, nobody wants to eat bitter burnt garlic. Watch cooking time as they burn easily.

10. Serve in a bowl and garnish with scallions, sliced boiled eggs, and roasted garlic toppings.

11. Garnish with ground black pepper, splash of soy sauce, and a lemon wedge. Enjoy!

Chapter 5

---◆---

IS IT TIME TO EAT YET?
BEEF DISHES

Dad's beef dishes always required lots of patience on my part. Growing up, it was the worst. I would drive my family crazy asking if it was time to eat yet? He would boil these dishes for hours until it was just tender enough. Not too much or it loses texture and flavor. Later in my adult life, dad started using pressure cookers and Instapots more and more. I dare say that using these techniques felt like cheating. Call me traditional but there was something magical about the aroma of beef dishes developing throughout the house all day then finally getting to feast on it at dinner time. The experience is beyond gratifying. At the end of the meal, you look into that empty bowl and feel justified in saying "I slayed that dragon!"

IS IT TIME TO EAT YET? BEEF DISHES

Beef Nilaga (Beef Bone Soup)

Serves: 4   Prep time: 10 mins Cook time: 3 hours

Nilaga (Nee-lah-gah) is to boil. Boiling is dad's secret ingredient for developing flavors of love in this dish. Beef Nilaga to me means long conversations with my dad. Many of my life decisions were made boiling this beef soup. Nilaga, this is my love letter to you, my dear friend.

There is a dish called Beef Bulalo (Bul-la-lo) that shares this recipe. Beef Bulalo has bone marrow in the bone while Beef Nlilaga does not.

INGREDIENTS

4 cups water

2 pounds beef shank

4 cloves garlic (chopped)

1 medium yellow onion
(chopped)

2 tablespoons whole black
pepper

4 russet potatoes (peeled and
quarter cubed)

4 medium carrots (1/2 inch)

1 teaspoon fish sauce or more
to taste

1 cube beef bouillon or 1
tablespoon beef seasoning

½ cabbage whole leaf
(individually detached)

1 thumb ginger

1/2 cup green onions (1 1/2-
inch)

2 ears of corn (cut into fours)

½ pound green beans (2
inches)

1 bundle bok choy (halved)

DIRECTIONS

1. Add water to a big pot and let it boil.
2. Add the beef shank, garlic, onion and whole black pepper, then simmer for 2 hours or until meat is tender.
3. Add the potatoes. Simmer until almost tender.
4. Add the fish sauce, beef bouillon or seasoning, carrots, cabbage, green onion, corn, green beans, and bok choy. Cook until carrots are slightly tender.
5. Serve with a small plate of soy sauce with lemon juice to dip the beef and vegetables in before every warm bite. Enjoy!

Beef Kaldereta (Filipino Beef Stew)

Serves: 6   Prep time: 10 mins Cook time: 3 hours

Kaldereta (Kal-der-re-ta) is Filipino tomato-based beef stew. "Caldera" is a Spanish word for large cooking pot. Kaldereta is a large pot of stew. Dad traditionally made this dish with goat meat. But goat meat is not children approved so I'm including my beef recipe. Substitute goat for beef if you wish to experience more traditional flavors. This dish is hearty, rich, and is a staple in Filipino cuisine.

INGREDIENTS

¼ cup neutral oil (canola or vegetable)

1 large carrot (cubed)

2 large potato (cubed)

4 pounds beef short ribs

1 head garlic (chopped)

2 large yellow onion (chopped)

½ teaspoon salt or more to taste

¼ teaspoon ground black pepper or more to taste

14 ounces tomato sauce

1 cube beef bouillon or 1 tablespoon beef seasoning

2 pounds of beef stock

1 cup liver spread

2 medium red bell pepper (sliced)

1 cup manzanilla olives (jarred or canned)

DIRECTIONS

1. Heat oil in a big pot.

2. Fry the carrots for 2 minutes or until all sides are cooked equally and browned. Set aside.

3. Fry the potato until cooked equally and brown. Set aside.

4. Add beef short ribs and rotate until browned.

5. Add garlic and onion with salt and pepper and sauté until onions are soft and translucent.

6. Add tomato sauce and beef bouillon or seasoning. Stir for 1 minute to loosen the beef bouillon.

7. Add beef stock. Bring to a boil then cover the pot and adjust to low heat. Slow cook the stew until the beef is falling off the bone and tenderizes completely. About 2 hours.

8. Add liver spread and stir for 3 minutes to distribute evenly.

9. Add cooked carrot and potato, red pepper and green olives until red pepper is slightly cooked.

10. Serve and enjoy!

Beef Kare Kare (Peanut Butter Beef Stew)

Serves: 6   Prep time: 15 mins   Cook time: 4 hours

Kare Kare (Karh-eh Karh-eh) is oxtail beef stewed in peanut butter. Can we say anaphylactic for both my children? I always kept an epinephrine pen near me when we would have this on our dinner table. However, this dish, when safe for lucky peanut eaters like me, is delectable. While it is bold and rich in flavor, it is apparently not bold enough for the Filipino palates. Kare Kare lovers add sautéed Bagoong, fermented shrimp paste, as a condiment. This is the same shrimp paste seen in Pinakbet except this version is sautéed with garlic for extra yummy powers. Don't let this side paste scare you away, give it a taste. This recipe, however, is equally scrumptious with or without the controversial Bagoong.

INGREDIENTS

1 liter water

3 pounds oxtail (cut in 2 inch slices. You can also use tripe or a combination of both)

1 cup ground peanuts

½ cup smooth peanut butter

½ cup annatto powder (soaked in ½ cup of water for red coloring)

1 tablespoon fish sauce

½ teaspoon salt or more to taste

¼ teaspoon ground black pepper

½ cup toasted ground rice

¼ cup neutral oil (canola or vegetable)

1 tablespoon garlic (minced)

1 medium yellow onion (chopped)

4 Japanese eggplant (sliced)

10 string beans (2 inch)

½ pound bok choy (halved)

DIRECTIONS

1. Boil water in a large pot.

2. Add oxtail and onions. Simmer for 3.5 hours or until the meat is tender. If using a pressure cooker, usually will take only 35 minutes.

3. Once the meat is tender, add the ground peanuts, peanut butter, and liquid annatto. Simmer for 5 minutes.

4. Add fish sauce, salt, and pepper to taste. Simmer for 2 minutes.

5. Add the toasted ground rice. Simmer for 5 minutes until it is time to add the cooked vegetables.

6. In a separate medium pan, heat oil and sauté garlic and onion for 3 minutes or until onion is soft and translucent.

7. Add eggplant, string beans, and bok choy. Cook for 5 minutes or until just tender.

8. To the simmering pot of beef, add lightly cooked vegetables. Gently mix, careful not to break the eggplant.

9. Serve hot with rice and sauteed bagoong shrimp paste for daring enthusiasts.

Beef Tapa (Marinated Beef)

Serves: 4 Prep time: 12 mins Cook time: 25 min
Marination time: 12 hours

Tapa (Tap-pa) is thinly sliced beef marinated in sweet, salty, and citrus flavors that is then pan fried dry to perfection. It is my son's favorite dish. How do I know? Every time I make this dish, he gives me a side teenage hug, thanks me for making dinner and tells me he loves me. I cannot help but beam with glee in knowing that in that two-minute window of time, I am his favorite person. I will take it!

INGREDIENTS

1 ½ pound beef sirloin
thinly sliced

3 tablespoon garlic
(minced)

5 tablespoons soy sauce

½ cup freshly squeezed
lemon juice

¼ teaspoon salt

2 tablespoon white sugar

¼ teaspoon ground
black pepper

3 tablespoons neutral oil
(canola or vegetable)

DIRECTIONS

1. Place the beef in the clear plastic bag.
2. In it, add garlic, soy sauce, lemon juice, salt, sugar, pepper and mix well. Set aside.
3. Place inside the refrigerator and marinate for a minimum of 12 hours.
4. After 12 hours of marinating, drain the beef from the marinade. Save the marinade.
5. Heat oil in a medium pan.
6. Add marinated beef including the marinade juices until beef is cooked and tender. About 15-20 minutes depending on the cut of the meat.
7. Cook until the water evaporates and beef fries dry.
8. Serve and enjoy!

Chapter 6

SPEAK TO MY SOUL PORK DISHES

Filipinos take pride in pork or "baboy" dishes. In the very heart and soul of Philippine culture is Lechon. Lechon is a whole roasted pig which is often a centerpiece for festive occasions, celebrations, or large gatherings. In its very essence, lechon is iconic for epitomizing joy and unity.

Dishes like sauteed pig ears and sizzling sisig made typically from chopped pork parts like jowl, ears, cheeks, liver, and pork belly, ensure that no part of lechon goes to waste. My brother loves his sisig. Considered a "pulutan" (appetizer or snacks), sisig is served on a sizzling hot plate. Think sizzling fajitas but with pork and only pork. He pairs it with his favorite beer and with every bite reminds me how much he loves this dish. I wish that I knew how to make sisig so that I could share it with you in this book.

Filipinos absolutely adores crunchy pork. Favored dishes that gloriously deliver a salty crunch include Lechon Kawali (roasted pork belly) or Crispy Pata (deep fried pork knuckles). Do not knock it until you try it.

Chapter 6

---◆---

SPEAK TO MY SOUL PORK DISHES

Lechong Paksiw (Lechon Stew)

Serves: 4   Prep time: 5 mins   Cook time: 15 mins

The best part of having lechon leftovers is lechon Paksiw (Pah-k-si-w). Paksiw means to cook and simmer in vinegar. This traditional dish is humble yet mouthwatering. In fact, some would say that the purpose of having a lechon is to have enough leftovers to make this dish. If we only eat with our eyes, however, I am not sure if this dish will gain loyal followers. If you can bypass its non glamourous grey stew appearance, you are in for an expedition of flavors.

INGREDIENTS

2 tablespoons neutral oil (canola or vegetable)

3 cloves garlic (minced)

1 medium yellow onion (sliced)

2 pounds leftover pork lechon

1 cup water

¼ cup white vinegar

¾ tablespoon salt

½ teaspoon whole peppercorn

4 dried bay leaves

1 pound liverwurst

1 tablespoon brown sugar

DIRECTIONS

1. Heat oil in a large pot.
2. Sauté onion for 2 minutes until onion is soft and translucent. Add garlic and cook for 1 minute until soft.
3. Add leftover lechon and cook until lightly brown.
4. Add water and let it simmer for 2 minutes.
5. Pour vinegar and let it boil for 3 minutes.
6. Add salt, peppercorn, and bay leaves. Stir and let it simmer for another 3 minutes.
7. Add liverwurst until fully melted and incorporated evenly into the dish.
8. Add sugar and simmer until sauce thickens.
9. Serve and enjoy!

Pork Tocino (Caramelized Savory Pork)

Serves: 6

Prep time: 1 hour
Marination time: 12 hours

Cook time: 50 min

Tocino (Toh-sin-no) is a sweet and savory pork dish. Marinated pork slices are pan fried into glistening caramelized red pork. It smells and tastes of sweet, sour, and garlic. I must warn you that this dish uses red food coloring which means wear gloves during preparation or your hands will be stained red for days. Has anyone tried making this dish without the food coloring? Good question! The answer from me and my family is no, we haven't tried because what is Tocino if not for the glistening red meat I just described in full admiration.

INGREDIENTS

3 cloves garlic (finely minced)

1 ½ tablespoons salt

¾ cup brown sugar

½ tablespoons finely ground
black pepper

1 tablespoon rice flour

1 tablespoon soy sauce

2 tablespoons rice vinegar

¼ cup pineapple juice

2 tablespoons red food color

2 pounds pork butt or shoulder
(¼ inch thin)

1 cup water

3 tablespoon neutral oil (canola
or vegetable)

DIRECTIONS

1. Combine and mix all ingredients in a glass bowl, except for the pork slices, water and oil.

2. Add the pork slices and mix all ingredients using your hands (wear gloves to avoid stains).

3. Place in a sealable zip lock bag and marinade in the refrigerator overnight.

4. Remove from the refrigerator. Use gloves to mix ingredients again several times before returning in the refrigerator. Cure for 1-3 days.

5. After curing, add water and oil into medium pan and bring to a boil.

6. Add marinated pork. Do not overcrowd the pan or pork will steam and not caramelize.

7. Adjust the heat to medium and cook until the water evaporates. Continue to fry until pork caramelizes.

8. Serve and enjoy!

Lomi Soup (Egg Noodle Soup with Meatballs)

Serves: 4   Prep time: 10 mins Cook time: 50 mins

Lomi (Loh-me) is a type of thick egg noodle that is thicker than pancit canton. Lomi soup is a hearty dish that my family traditionally eats every Christmas eve before opening presents. This may be an unconventional recipe because I only know my dad's Lomi. My favorite part of this soup is biting into imperfectly hand formed pork meatballs. If you have ever compared a hamburger from a restaurant with perfectly formed patties to one with hand formed patties, you will know what I mean by these meatballs. There is just something intimate and loving about knowing the preparer took care to laboriously make fresh hand formed meatballs. Lomi soup is simply the dish that feels like a warm embrace during a dark and cold winter night.

INGREDIENTS

1 pound ground pork

2 eggs

½ cup flour

8 cloves garlic (minced)

1/2 thumb ginger (minced)

1 medium yellow onion (minced)

½ teaspoon salt or more to taste

¼ teaspoon ground black pepper
or more to taste

3 tablespoons neutral oil (canola
or vegetable)

5 cups water

2 cubes chicken bouillon or 2
tablespoons chicken seasoning

12 ounces lomi noodles

3 Chinese sausages (sliced
diagonally)

1/2 pound of fish balls (halved)

1 small cabbage (shredded)

1 ½ tablespoons cornstarch

2 eggs

DIRECTIONS

1. Combine the ground pork, egg, flour, half of the minced garlic, ginger, half of the minced onion, salt and ground black pepper in a bowl and mix. Set aside.

2. Heat oil in a large pot.

3. Sauté the remaining garlic and the remaining onion until the onions are soft and translucent.

4. Add 5 cups of water and let it boil.

5. Add chicken bouillon in the boiling water.

6. Take the mixed meat mixture and scoop one heaping tablespoon of the mixture and form a meat ball with your hand. Drop in the soup. Repeat until all the pork is formed into a meat ball and dropped into the soup.

7. Cook for 10 minutes or until meatballs are cooked through.

8. Add noodles, Chinese sausage, fish balls, cabbage and stir. Cook for about 5 minutes.

9. Mix cornstarch and ½ cup water and completely blend. Add into the pot and stir continuously until the soup thickens.

10. Scramble the egg into a bowl and slowly pour the egg into the soup while mixing the soup to allow the egg to cook into thin elongated egg droplets.

11. Garnish with siracha or your hot sauce for a little kick.

12. Ladle into a lucky bowl and enjoy!

Pork Sinigang (Sour Tamarind Soup)

Serves: 4   Prep time: 10 mins Cook time: 1 hour

Nothing says Filipino cuisine like Pork Sinigang (Sin-eh-gang). This dish is most definitely unique to Filipino cuisine for its distinctive sour taste from the likes of tamarind. If the sourness of this dish does not make you pucker on the first bite, it has failed its mission. I wish that I could share with you how to make it from scratch, but this was one of the few dishes that dad allowed a cheat. There are these miraculous packets of Sinigang powder available for purchase. My poor aunt has made the mistake of adding just one packet of powder to the Sinigang dish she served the family. Let us just say, she will never make that mistake again. We love our sour. Since then, you will see her bringing extra packets of sinigang powder just in case she reads the room and decides that there is not enough puckering going on.

The secret to this dish? Tomato. When the tomatoes melt into the broth, it adds a depth of tartness that makes this soup even more scrumptious. If you dare, double the tomato ingredient.

INGREDIENTS

4 cups water

2 pounds pork ribs (cut into serving pieces)

4 tomatoes (quarter cut)

1 medium yellow onion (quarter cut)

1 tablespoon fish sauce

4 medium taro roots (peeled and quartered)

1 Japanese eggplant (cut into 1-inch pieces)

1 medium daikon radish (diagonal)

10 string beans (2 inches)

8 okras (trim ends)

1 packet sinigang powder or more to taste

2 whole jalapeno

1/2 pound kangkong or water spinach (if available or use fresh spinach)

DIRECTIONS

1. In a large pot, place water and boil over high heat.

2. Add pork ribs and let it boil. Remove the residue that floats to the surface using a spoon. Boil for 5 minutes.

3. Add tomatoes, onion and fish sauce. Cover the pot with the lid and adjust the heat to low heat and let it cook for 25 minutes or until meat becomes tender.

4. Once tender, add taro root and eggplant. Cover and simmer again for 5 minutes or until taro pieces are tender.

5. Add daikon radish, string beans, and okra. Cover and let it simmer for 2 minutes until just tender

6. Add the packet of sinigang powder broth until dissolved and jalapeno. Simmer for 2 minutes. Pierce the jalapeno if you want a spicy kick.

7. Turn off the heat and add kangkong leaves. Let the leaves cook from the residual heat.

8. Serve hot and enjoy!

Chapter 7

I SHOULDN'T BUT I WILL DESSERTS

If I had to choose a category of food that is most unique to the Philippine cuisine, I would select the dessert category. I can go to a Chinese or Spanish restaurant to look for the flavors of the Philippine cuisine and find similarities. But when it comes to our desserts, our flavor profiles and textures are unique and harder to find in other cuisines.

I remember most people at our parties being overly satiated from our vast spread of food that when the dessert table was populated with dessert dishes, it was met with grunts from the pressure of having to eat more. Some people would deny the dessert table all together and simply refuse to take another bite. We usually see these people at the dessert table within half an hour. Others, the warriors among us, would unbuckle a notch on their belt and say: "I shouldn't but I will."

I SHOULDN'T BUT I WILL DESSERTS

Turon (Plantain Banana Fried Eggroll)

Serves: 6   **Prep time: 10 mins** **Cook time: 12 mins**

Turon (Too-run) was my dad's favorite dessert. He could never resist it and could never eat just one. Turon is to take a sliced banana, plantain banana was the preferred choice, wrap it in lumpia wrapper, and deep fry into this delectable crispy treat. I have seen people substitute banana with sweet potato. Both are equally delicious.

Have you ever watched the show Carnival Eats from the Cooking Channel? I am a fan of the show because I am intrigued about what people can coat and deep fry. I have always wanted to try the deep-fried cheesecake! This concept is what turon reminds me of. Stuff lumpia wrappers with anything sweet, roll, deep fry then voila, a simple dessert that packs a crispy punch of happiness. Is it carnival eats worthy? Try for yourself and let me know!

INGREDIENTS

1 1/2 cup sugar

6 plantain banana slices (half lengthwise)

1 cup jack fruit ripe (sliced)

12 pieces lumpia wrapper

1 cup neutral oil (canola or vegetable)

DIRECTIONS

1. Add sugar on a plate and roll the banana to fully coat with sugar.
2. Place the sugar-coated banana on the lumpia wrapper and add a slice of ripe jackfruit on top.
3. See page 9 for instructions on "How To Roll A Lumpia."
4. Roll unfried lumpia in the plate of sugar. Set aside.
5. Heat the oil in a frying pan.
6. Fry lumpia for 2 minutes or until golden brown. You will see some caramelization outside the fried lumpia from the sugar it was rolled on.
7. Serve and enjoy the sweet crunch!

Halo-Halo (Mixed Medley of Ice, Milk, Sweets)

Serves: 1   Prep time: 5 mins   Cook time: 0 mins

Halo Halo (Ha-low Ha-low) means to mix and mix. This is the most recognized cold dessert in Philippine cuisine. While simple in its architecture of crushed ice and evaporated milk, makers of the dessert have an open range for creativity and individuality.

Creativity because added to the crushed ice and milk slurry can be sweet beans (red or white or both), chopped sweet fruits that are usually jarred, sweet corn kernels, Ube (purple yam) paste, leche flan, and any kind of ice cream such as mango or ube. Sweet fruits can be jackfruit, coconut, and tapioca jellies. Or, add any other toppings that are edible and sweet.

Individuality is what makes halo-halo so much fun to make and eat. My dad enjoyed it with only sweet corn kernels. My brother prefers only coconut pieces and kaong (jellybean shaped fruit from a sugar palm tree). My mom and I love to have all the toppings then end up sharing it because it is too much for one person.

This dessert is best consumed with a spoon because it is gloriously chunky with all its delightful ingredients. Mix it all together and indulge.

INGREDIENTS

1 teaspoon canned cream of corn

1 teaspoon store-bought jarred halo halo mixture of sweet red beans, nata de coco coconut jellies, and coconut strips

1 cup crushed ice or shaved ice

1 tablespoon leche flan (if available)

1 tablespoon ube purple root ice cream or paste (if available)

¼ cup canned evaporated milk

DIRECTIONS

1. Add a teaspoon of each of all the ingredients except for the ube jam or ube ice cream and leche flan in a tall glass.

2. Fill the glass with crushed ice and push it down to compact the crushed ice in the glass.

3. Top with ube jam or ube ice cream or leche flan

4. Drizzle milk as desired.

5. Serve with a long spoon and halo halo away!

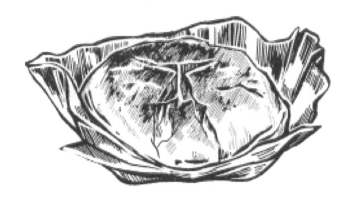

Bibingka - Baked Rice Cake in Banana Leaves

Serves: 4   Prep time: 10 mins Cook time: 25 mins

Bibingka (Bee-bing-kah) is a rice cake dessert that cooks in banana leaves. The cake is spongy from the gluten of the rice, lightly sweetened with coconut tones, and delightfully sticky. What is unique about this dessert is that it is sometimes paired with savory things such as a salty cured duck egg or shredded cheese. It is the most interesting and versatile dessert that you will crave for breakfast, lunch, and as a dinner dessert.

INGREDIENTS

1 cup rice flour

2 ½ teaspoon baking powder

½ teaspoon salt

4 tablespoons butter (melted)

½ cup granulated sugar

3 eggs

1 cup coconut milk

½ cup whole milk

4 pre-cut banana leaf

½ cup grated cheddar cheese

¼ cup grated coconut

DIRECTIONS

1. Pre-heat the oven to 375 °F.
2. Combine the dry ingredients of rice flour, baking powder, and salt in a bowl then set aside.
3. In another bowl, whisk together cooled 3 tablespoons melted butter, sugar, and eggs.
4. Slowly add the dry ingredients while continuing to whisk the wet ingredients.
5. Once incorporated, add coconut milk and whole milk and mix.
6. Line a 9x9" glass baking dish with pre-cut banana leaves.
7. Pour the mixture in the dish and bake for 15 minutes or until an inserted toothpick slides out clean from the center.
8. While hot, brush with remaining 1 tablespoon melted butter and add grated cheddar cheese on top of the bibingka.
9. Return the cooked bibingka in the oven and bake again for another 5 minutes or until the top of the bibingka turns medium brown.
10. Remove the bibingka from the oven and top with grated coconut.
11. Serve and enjoy!

Biko (Sweet Coconut Sticky Rice Squares)

Serves: 8   Prep time: 10 mins Cook time: 40 mins

Biko (bee-koh) is a rich, chewy, and sticky sweet rice. When plated, it is usually cut into squares like brownies.

What do you get when you take rice and cook it with coconut milk and brown sugar? You get a dense and sticky sweet rice with a luxurious caramel topping. This dessert is a stick to the roof of your mouth goodness that easily makes this a family favorite.

INGREDIENTS

2 cups glutinous rice or
sticky rice

1 ½ cups water

4 1/2 cups coconut milk (3 cans)

2 1/2 cups brown sugar

1 teaspoon salt

DIRECTIONS

1. Cook the sticky rice with water in a rice cooker. If you do not have a rice cooker, cook rice in a pot over the stovetop following instructions from the rice packaging.

2. Meanwhile, in a separate pot, combine coconut milk, brown sugar, and salt. Cook in low heat and continuously stir until it becomes thick.

3. Remove half of the simmering coconut milk and brown sugar syrup to set aside. This will be the finishing topping.

4. To the simmering coconut milk and brown sugar syrup, add cooked rice. Continue cooking and mixing until liquid evaporates being careful not to overcook and burn the bottom. This is biko.

5. Place the cooked biko into 8" x 8" glass baking dish. Spread to evenly distribute and flatten the surface.

6. Pour the remaining half of the syrup that is set aside over the biko. Spread evenly as a topping.

7. Cut into squares, serve and enjoy!

Chapter 8

PANDESAL

Pandesal (Pahn-de-sahl) is the most popular bread roll in the Philippines. It has an interesting bread crumb coating around the shell but when you break into it, it is soft and fluffy and mildly sweet. It is commonly eaten for breakfast or merienda. My family devours these rolls with the lomi soup every year on Christmas eve. While lomi reminds me of Christmas eve, pandesal reminds me of the loving embrace that overwhelmed me when my children remembered papa's bread.

Pandesal (Filipino Bread Rolls)

Serves: 12   Prep time: 10 mins   Cook time: 15 mins

You didn't think that I would forget the very recipe which inspired this book project did you? And now, the pièce de résistance! The bread that brought me back to the land of hope. The same bread that when my children closed their eyes to fully admire its scent, felt a warm hug from their papa.

Here is the recipe for Pandesal, our coveted bread roll. A national treasure. Please handle it with special care and love in your heart. Once you have taken it out of the oven, tear a hot bun in half and allow it to melt your heart. I cannot wait for you to experience what I mean by this! I dare say, you are welcome.

INGREDIENTS

1 cup whole milk (lukewarm)

1 ½ teaspoon instant dry yeast

3 cups all-purpose flour

1 teaspoon salt

¼ cup sugar

2 tablespoon butter (melted)

1 egg (beaten)

1 tablespoon neutral oil (canola or vegetable)

¼ cup bread crumbs

DIRECTIONS

1. Combine warm whole milk with 1 ½ teaspoon instant dry yeast in a bowl and set aside to activate the yeast.

2. In a separate large bowl, mix the dry ingredients flour, salt and sugar.

3. Into the bowl of dry ingredients, add the active yeast, cooled melted butter, and beaten egg. Mix until well incorporated.

4. On a floured surface, place the dough and knead repeatedly for 10 minutes until it becomes smooth and elastic.

5. Form a ball shaped dough and coat with a small amount of oil. Put it in a bowl, cover with a towel and place it in a warm area. Wait for it to rise until it doubled in size. This could take 30 minutes to an hour depending on the room temperature.

6. Once doubled in size, punch down the dough and divide or slice into two equal portions. Roll each half into a log shape. Cut each log into six equal pieces.

7. Roll each piece into balls. Then, roll each balls around in breadcrumbs to cover all the sides.

8. Place buns on baking sheet lined with parchment paper. Keep buns one inch apart for room to grow. Cover buns with a towel and leave in a warm area. Let rise until double in size in about 30 minutes to an hour depending on the room temperature.

9. Preheat over for 375 °F.

10. Bake for 15-20 minutes until golden brown.

11. While fresh out of the oven, enjoy this treat with a steaming hot beverage.

Conclusion

Thank you for allowing me to share this Filipino culinary journey with you. A celebration of my life with dad in the kitchen.

The sudden event of losing a core person who was such an integral part of my life killed a piece of me. By surviving the dark clouds of grief and finding hope through cooking dad's dishes, I am a new version of myself. Even though the life that I lead is not my preferred version. I prefer to walk through life with my dad physically beside me. I am newly awakened. Life, my life, your life, our life, indeed is a gift. We only get one and it is temporary. Luckily, dad left me with many loving memories. He inspires me to do the same with my own children. Since my time here on earth includes mortality, I have come to realize that the only path worth taking is those that end with love, joy, and connection.

I hope this book inspires you to explore Philippine cuisine in your own home with your own loved ones. Most of all, I hope it serves as a catalyst for making happy and fulfilling memories.

Now, Kain na tayo (Kah-in nah tah-yo) or lets eat!

Your feedback is greatly appreciated!

It's through your feedback, support and reviews that I'm able to create the best books possible and serve more people.

I would be extremely grateful if you could take just 60 seconds to kindly leave an honest review of the book on Amazon. Please share your feedback and thoughts for others to see.

To do so, simply find the book on Amazon's website (or wherever you purchased the book from) and locate the section to leave a review. Select a star rating and write a couple of sentences.

That's it! Thank you so much for your support.

Review this product

Share your thoughts with other customers

Write a customer review

Made in United States
Troutdale, OR
12/20/2024

26941169R00051